T0115083

love is eternal

Vicki Case

BALBOA
PRESS

A DIVISION OF HAY HOUSE

Balboa Press books may be ordered through booksellers or by contacting:

Balboa Press
A Division of Hay House
1663 Liberty Drive
Bloomington, IN 47403
www.balboapress.com.au
1-(877) 407-4847

ISBN: 978-1-4525-0620-3 (sc)
ISBN: 978-1-4525-0623-4 (e)

Printed in the United States of America

Balboa Press rev. date: 07/16/2012

Epigraph

'Poetry is not an opinion. It is a song that rises
from a bleeding wound or a smiling mouth'

Kahlil Gibran; *Sand & Foam*

Dedication

This book is dedicated to the amazing man who taught me to, not only love again, but to love and believe in myself; my beloved Eros.

Although he has chosen a different path for his life, he will forever reside in my heart.

Acknowledgements

I would like to thank those people who have supported and encouraged me in writing this book. First and foremost there is the extraordinary man I fell in love with (my Eros) who encouraged me to believe in myself and told me that my work was good and that it should be published.

Thanks must also go to my beautiful parents (Kelvin and Dawn) who have unfailingly supported me in everything that I have ever done, although they have not always agreed with some of the decisions I have made.

Finally I want to thank my dearest friends Michelle Myers, Carol Hawthorn and Sue Dunn who have been there for me through the difficulties I have endured in losing the only man I have ever really loved. They have all been towers of strength and stability for me. I am forever indebted to them all.

Preface

Sometimes someone comes along and changes your life forever. My life changed forever in 2007 when fate bought a man, who was to become the love of my life, and I together. I was going through a very difficult time. I simply existed in an unhappy marriage, veiling my misery and unhappiness from the world with a smile. Although family and friends believed I had the perfect marriage, it was truly a farce.

This man came along and had a profound affect on me. He saw something in me that others didn't or couldn't see. He not only saw it, but he took the time to nurture it and watch it grow.

I am the confident and successful woman I am today because of him, the faith he had in me and the encouragement he gave me. He once said to me, words to the effect of:

'Even a neglected seedling, properly nurtured and cared for, can blossom into a beautiful flower'.

Because I was unhappy and lacked any self confidence or self esteem, I found myself seeking him out for guidance, advice and, if I am totally honest, a degree of attention. As a result of this, a strong bond and friendship was soon forged between us. I found myself divulging to him things that I had never told another living soul. He truly does know all of my inner most secrets. I have never trusted another human being enough before to disclose the things I have revealed to him.

I soon realised that I had developed a strong emotional attachment for him, which I fought internally for many years. We were both married and a relationship was forbid.

In April 2009, after finding enough internal fortitude to leave a loveless and emotionally abusive marriage I told him of the feelings I had for him. To my complete and utter surprise he did not push me away however he did reinforce the boundaries, and our friendship grew stronger.

Then, in the winter of 2010, and after my decree nici, I received an unexpected phone call one afternoon. I drove to his work, met with him and the rest is history.

I gave him the pet name 'Eros'. He is my God of love and, to this day, I adore and worship the ground that he walks on. I began composing some ad hoc words (poems) to indicate how I felt about him and would SMS one to him each morning. He used to tell me that he was flattered by my words, and that my poetry was good, and that I should publish it.

Eros is, and will always be, the only love of my life. I have never loved like this before, nor do I envisage I ever will again. Losing my beloved Eros was worse than anything else in my life that I have ever experienced. After he severed our relationship, with an impersonal SMS I spiraled into the depths of depression. Only my doctor and a few very close friends ever knew the extent of my love, grief and depression.

One way in which I dealt with my loss and the emotional and physical effects on me from my grief was through continuing to write my poetry. This time however I modified my poems to reflect the feelings and emotions I was experiencing during this dark period in my life.

The contents of my (now) three poetry books; Unconditional Forbidden Love; A Journey of Hurt—Captured in Ink; and this book contain the poems I initially sent to him about my love for him and then; subsequent, poems about the ebb and flow of my feelings as a result of losing him and the grief and mourning I have since endured.

The poems in my books depict my journey of love, loss and sacrifice

Table of Contents

Your Words Hurt

I was so hurt
The day you called
Angry at me and said
You were appalled.

Accused me of causing you
Grief from my contact
She had seen my words; and
It had had an impact.

I wasn't to know
An email shared
Or that she'd see
My words I still cared.

I wanted to hold you
To the promise you made
You'd stay in touch; and
Our memories never fade.

I'd never hurt you
I'd hurt myself first
Your words of anger
They were the worst.

I wasn't to know
It'd bring you grief
In reality however
It was probably a relief.

Crying Alone

There isn't a day
I don't think of you
Without you my love
I remain always blue.

I'm tired of crying
When you don't care
Loving you handsome
Was a one sided affair.

I'm so damn tired
Of crying on the inside
All the time pretending
To smile on the outside.

You sit all alone
Alone in a room
Watching the football
Your life now gloom.

You call now and then
For seconds at a time
Taken when you can
Without getting in a bind.

If you are just
Covering your arse and bases
Gone will be
All my airs and graces.

I Still Love You

When I close my eyes
You are the only one I see
The nights I've cried over you
Wishing you were here with me

I love you to my very being
But today
There's nothing to smile about
Since you walked away

You are the object
Of my entire passion
Yet you cut me loose
Without showing any compassion

I've finally realised
That you didn't love me
It was just sex
That's all it was to thee

I've done my utmost
To ensure your protection
As I vowed I always would
Despite your rejection

But I need to see you
Just once more
Before my life ends
Standing at my door

Your Photograph

I can't erase memories
That mean so much
I'm dying on the inside
Longing for your touch.

There's a photo of you
Next to my bed
Sitting there proudly
Next to my head.

I talk to your photo
So that you can hear
I tell you I love you; and
You should never fear.

Your eyes they stare at me
Like yours once did
So beautiful and green
They can't be hid.

You are extraordinary
I am in awe of you
My love for you is eternal
Nothing could be more true.

I can't ever imagine
Loving someone else
The way that I love you
Not even myself.

Heartbroken & lost looking at my photograph of Eros

My Debut

I remember vividly
When I made my debut
Singing on stage
Singing for you

That afternoon
Alone and scared
You texted good luck
My fear you shared

The text was unexpected
But it meant a great deal
Although the moment to send
You had to steal

Your actions say you care
Over and over they came
Although you confessed
You felt guilt and shame

Your words said one thing
Your actions yet another
Perhaps your arse
You were looking to cover

Whatever the reason
Your words were profound
They gave me courage; and
Made my heart pound

Vicki singing with Michelle Myers & Celebration Mix.
Photograph by: Dawn Case

Why?

I am an amazing woman
Who deserved much more
To be treated better by you
Not discarded on the floor

I have since been told
I'm not the first
With whom you've strayed
Before the bubble burst

But I stand alone now
Looking out at nothing
For me my love
It was more than a fling

I gave you everything
I held nothing back
Even prepared to take
All incoming flack

The only man in my life now
Is my faithful cattle dog
However unlike you now
My affection he wants to hog

Me

What could I possibly give you?
That you don't already possess
Just a love that's deep and true
That no other can ever address

I definitely don't need
To reside in a prestigious place
Or drive a classy automobile
Just so I can have face

Nor do I need
To be given everything
All things that open and shut
Or to amass rings and bling

I don't need status
Just to be someone
This you must know
If you're ever to come

I don't need eminence
I am just who I am
I am a unique individual
Don't need to be 'one of them'

That's what you saw in me
Someone pure of heart
That's why you came to me; and
A relationship we did start

The Tears I Still Cry

My eyes they are closed
But the tears they still stream
My room is so dark
Not even a light beam

No matter what I do
The tears they won't stop
But for you however
My love is now forgot

I miss you handsome
I still miss you so; but
I'm not allowed to say it
People think I'm a nut

You never really cared
About my hopes and dreams
Or you wouldn't have hurt me
Or that's how it seems

You were my rock
Until you crushed me
Without any remorse
Why can't you see?

When You Call

I look forward to contact
From you when you can
It's like winning lotto
You'll always be my man

Do you have any idea?
Just how much I hurt
When I tell you '*I love you*'; and
You laugh at me curt

Before she found out
I'd declare my love for you
You'd smile and say
I know you do

So what has changed?
I can tell from your voice
The calls are a chore
Not made by choice

That just leaves fear
Of what I might do
I just don't understand
I'd never hurt you

It just goes to show
You don't have a clue
What was offered you?
Now we're both so blue

Love is Eternal

My love is eternal
And you are a fool
You could have had it all
But you gave up a jewel

A jewel that's so special
Not to mention amazing
I could have been yours
Yours for the taking

It hurt when you ended it
The way that you did
So cowardly and insensitive
Something I'd expect from a kid

I know I should tell you
To leave me alone
I hurt so much each time
You call me on the phone

I know that I should but
The words won't come out
Each time you hang up
I just want to shout

I've written you a letter
Telling you goodbye
I don't have the courage
To send it and I cry

Wish Upon A Star

One solitary star
Alone in the night sky
Upon which to wish
You'd never said goodbye

My wishes go unanswered
So many I have made
They're all the same however
I am so afraid

Afraid that I've lost you
Lost you forever
But I'll just never know
Like tomorrow's weather

Everything has its time
That's what I'm told
You and I had ours
Now we're alone and cold

Each night I ask the Angels
To lead you back to me
Only time will tell
I'll just wait and see

I pray you come to your senses
And realise what could be
We are incredible together
Yet you hold the only key

My 'Eros' Tattoo

I'd sacrifice my life for you
But not my beliefs
My love for you handsome
Now tattooed motifs

They're a constant reminder
Of the love we once shared
I'll never forget you
Despite how I faired

It's tattooed on my chest
On top of my heart
Each time I see it
I cry we're still apart

Along with my memories
It's all I have left
Your name now embossed
Upon my left breast

'Satan'

You have no idea
Of the journey I've travelled
I've lived in hell; and
With Satan I've dabbled

He went out of his way
And offered me a deal
Give him my heart and soul; and
My wish will become real

His offer was generous
And consider it I did
But not even for you
Could I agree to his bid?

He turned up the heat
My soul the ultimate prize
But even for you handsome
The price he'd have to rise

To have you as mine
I'd sacrifice a great deal
Satan tested my love; and
It reinforced how I feel

I never gave in
Despite the temptation
My love for you handsome is
A deep love and total adoration

You Broke My Heart

My heart is a mess
Since you broke it in two
Not even a transplant
Could restore it to its hue

Of all the men
To have crossed my path
You're the last I'd thought
Would discard me on the hearth

Now I can't find solace
No matter what I do
Nor can I find peace
Since the day I lost you

You vowed to never hurt me
But devastate me you did
I don't think I'll ever recover
I feel so utterly stupid

Stupid to have loved you
A fool to still care
But for the time we shared
We made one hell of a pair

You can't deny handsome
The connection we felt
Making love with each other
We'd fuse together and melt

Vicki; broken hearted at the loss of her beloved Eros

Alone

As I stare out now
Into the black darkness
I know how you feel
This illness called stress

You feel so alone
The walls closing in
It's like everything
Has become a cardinal sin

Some offer their help
But don't really mean it
Others shy away; and
Don't give a shit

A few will be there
To offer their support
But even they're not sure
And some will abort

One or maybe two
Their concerns will be true
That's what I am handsome
A friend always to you

Although you can't see it now
I am always here for you
But you don't realise this
Because you're sick and blue

'Susie'

Susie is a dear friend
A friend through and through
We met in 1975; and
Our friendship it grew

We've both had bad patches
That life throws at us all
Susie was always there
And never let me fall

We've shared funny times
Not to mention some sad
But we always got through them
And didn't go stark raving mad

Susie was my strength
Not to mention a great support
When I left my husband
Who was a ripe tort?

Then she was there again
When Eros I found
She shared in my happiness
As my love it did abound

Again she was there
When Eros set me free
A pillar of strength and loyalty
She never just let me be

Forever True

Nothing will ever change
The love I have for you
It's etched in my heart; and
I remain forever true.

My heart it still beats
But it's lost all its lustre
Without you its rhythm
Is difficult to muster

You gave my life reason
You gave my heart hope
Since I lost you handsome
All I do is mope

My eyes are always swollen
Blood shot and red
That because they're so sad
From the tears they've shed

I pray nightly to the Angels
To bring you back to me
I've even summoned God
To try and make you see

But I am still waiting
I guess the time isn't right
To be together again; and
Our futures forever bright

'Gorgeous'

You used to call me 'Gorgeous'
That now I really miss
All I get now is Vicki
'Gorgeous' relegated to the abyss

Verbally and in writing
It was 'Gorgeous' every time
It was like a pet name
That had replaced mine

Gone now is so much
All of which you can't fain
You can't blame it all
On your illness and pain

I've been wrong about many things
But not about you
You are a very special guy
I know this is so true

If you were just using me
You did a great job
I honestly thought you loved me
Not just pretending for a bob

Obviously I was an idiot
You; a good actor
Worthy of an academy award
I was fooled by your character

Goodbyes Hurt

Goodbyes; they always hurt
Your goodbye; it was the worst
The day you tore us apart
My heart shattered and burst

I pray that you regret it
Losing what bought you joy
Will you ever admit it?
Or forever remain coy

I've cried since I lost you
Much more than I should
Would you fix it handsome?
If in a flick you could

It is written in my eyes
And etched on my heart
I want and need you in my life
Never again; to be apart

I would rather have
A little piece of you
Than to live for all eternity
Without you at all; it's true

Touching You

Unbuttoning your shirt
For the very first time
I felt your heart racing
As too was mine

You felt so warm and soft
As my hand touched your chest
It went off on an adventure
Exploring all the rest

To look into your eyes
I paused from kissing you
You looked so happy and excited
This; experienced by too few

We had wasted too much time
Getting to this point
Let's not waste any more
Our love now let's anoint

We were together for hours
The passion it was intense
As the car windows they fogged
This was not some pretense

We had to part eventually
At least for today
You had to go home to her
Me; I was sent on my way

Holding Hands

One thing I really loved
Was holding your hand
It is so huge and strong
And never made a demand

Fitting together so perfectly
Designed to be held as one
It was so obvious to me
It was love; not just some fun

My fingers they always fitted
So snuggly into yours
Like they were manufactured
As one set of paws

Then pulled apart and sent forth
For fate to bring them together
Again but this time however
It would be for, forever

I always felt so safe
When our hands they entwined
I want to hold your hand forever
Never wanting them to unwind

I Want You Back

I pick up the phone
My hands they are shaking
I want to call you; but
You're not for the taking

I'm just prolonging the hurt
And extending my pain
You made your choice although
You had everything to gain

If you did come back
I'd always be second best
You made your decision; and
I don't want to be a pest

I am struggling; I admit it
With letting you go
You made a big mistake
But you don't yet know

One day you will wake up
And realise I really love you
What will you do then?
Me again; attempt to woo

When that day comes
Will you have the courage?
To make a wrong; right
You; I'd never dispourage

You!

I don't want another
If I can't have you
Won't settle for second best
No matter what they do

After loving you handsome
No other can compare
Your love and warmth
We are a perfect pair

If you are not hurting too
Then about you I was so wrong
Inside you must truly know
Together; we belong

I loved you handsome
Knowing you'd never be mine
Never asked you for anything
But with that I was fine

My love was unconditional
But I also challenged you too
Both mentally and emotionally
Please admit this to be true

The Prayer

God Our Father Almighty
Please listen to my prayer
About the man that I love; and
Whose life I long to share

He is going through a lot now
It's his health and other crap
Each time I try to reach out
It puts him in a flap

He used to relish my attention
Or that's what he would say
Now he's discarded me
Why do I now have to pay?

I was always faithful; and
Honest through and through
Never once let him down; and
All of this he knew

Why are we both to suffer so?
When others have done much worse
Are we both just unlucky?
Or is it some wicked curse

He doesn't deserve this
Neither to do I
We were great together
Now I'm left to ponder why

Forget Him

People they now beg me
To write about something else
You discovered my creative chakra
That had been hiding on the shelf

No one else inspires me
The way thoughts of you do
Perhaps they have never loved
With a love so deep and true

Some days are worse than others
Some days the words never stop
Some days I feel like
My head: it's going to pop

I find it so very easy
Writing poems of love and sin
Some people will read them
Others trashing them in the bin

But trash them or keep them
Deep inside me I know
At least I have the courage
To write and then them show

I've Cried

I've always cried in silence
I've always cried alone
Now I even cry some more
After you call me on the phone

I've used a hundred hankies
Not to mention a million tissues
Whilst you're probably happy; and
Never thought—*'miss you'*

I've cried inside a church
Cried and soaked the foot stool
Cried 'til I dehydrated; and
Realised I was a fool

I've cried while I was driving
The windscreen wipers didn't work
Cried 'til my face was drenched; and
Realised I was a jerk

But mostly I've cried
Cried tears on the inside
Cried when no one was looking
Cried since you texted goodbye

Have you even shed a tear?
Have you cried on the inside?
Have you ever regretted?
That insensitive SMS goodbye

Words Bombard Me

Sitting under the pergola
My dog by my side
The cat on my lap
Reliving; one hell of a ride

It had many highs; and
All too many lows
But I'd do it all again
Knowing how it goes

Imagine a B-52 bomber
Dropping its payload of bombs
That's how the words bombard me
But I remain always aplomb

Three books now I have written
About my love for you
What other man can say that?
And you don't have a clue

I need some respite
I'm drowning among the words
Words that are all about
The incredible love that you stirred

I love you more today
Then at any other time
Although it's been ten months
Since you cut the dreaded line

My Faithful Cattle Dog—'Patch'

Hurt and Anger

How can I hurt so much?
Yet not foster anger
It would be much easier
If you'd been just a stranger

Anger and hate
Won't bring you back
Nor will retaliation
Or any form of attack

You did what you did
Texting goodbye at the time
Thinking you were doing right; and
Definitely not a crime

I find myself defending you
At every turn and corner
Despite being left feeling like
A very sad close mourner

I asked you if I was a fool
To wit you replied 'no'
Was idiot a better descriptor?
Goes to show what you know

I Don't Want Revenge

My hearts been torn out
But I don't want revenge
Two wrongs don't make a right
Hence I won't avenge

How am I supposed to?
Get it through to you
That I love and need you
No matter what you do

You've asked me not to email
And to wait 'til you call
That doesn't leave many options
You've got a lot of gall

This way you have control
Holding all the aces
There's nothing I can do
To progress to other bases

I could disregard you
And initiate contact
You retain the upper hand
That's the sad fact

I know deep in my heart
Your contact will fade
Despite the promise
The promise that you made

Pandora's Box

So many words and feelings
That had been regressed
That is now words of poetry
That had been suppressed

Denigrated for decades
Convinced I should run and hide
Told I was good for nothing
And to this I should abide

You opened up Pandora's Box
Realised the treasure therein
Encouraged and supported me; and
Told me now a new start to begin

I've since achieved so much
And it's all because of you
You saw an amazing woman
Not a useless one; it's true

But then you disappeared
Vanished from my life
Went back to the sanctuary
With that of your second wife

One day I pray you will realise
What we could have done
If you'd had the courage; and
We'd united as one

I Should Thank You

I know that I should thank you
You've given me so much
Your love and lots of memories
From your kiss to your touch

Our time together was too short
Well far too short for me
You didn't seem to have a problem
Running from what could be

You scampered off so quickly
No time to say goodbye
Choose to tell me by an SMS
But forgot to mention why

If I'd not contacted you
Would you have stayed in touch?
As you did promise to me
Saying it wasn't asking too much

If you'd reconsidered and realised
That you'd promised me too much
You should have had the courage
To say you wouldn't stay in touch

You gave me a very lame excuse
Hoping that I'd accept it
But I'm just not that shallow
Not even a little bit

You've Changed

When you speak to me
You are so different now
It's like you're talking to
Your dog or the family cow

You said that I flattered you
And you loved the poems I wrote
Declaring my love and adoration
For you; no other bloke

Now you are so serious
You can't hang up fast enough
I don't get time to talk to you
About my life and other stuff

I feel like it's a chore for you
I've never felt that way before
Your calls used to leave me
Wanting you so much more

I miss what we used to have
I want it back so bad
But all I seem to do for you
Is make you really mad

Did I ever mean anything to you?
You made me think that I did
Have the courage to tell me
After all; I'm not a little kid

You!

33 poems now I've written
67 now I must find
To complete yet another book
The third poetry book of mine

I am changed forever today
Because you; you showed me
Many things; but mostly
What real love should be

The best days of my life
Were the days I spent with you?
Those fourteen months together
No words could be more true

I want to be with you
More than absolutely anything
I would do whatever you asked
If you'd simply ring

My body it still tingles
Whenever I think of you
Although it's been ten months
I'm so alone and blue

Even the smell that precedes
The impending rain
Reminds me of you; and
I'm not being deign

Both of You!

I remember the night
You took me to dinner
We both had a great time
I felt like a prize winner

We talked about everything
Dotted on each other's every word
Laughed a lot and aloud
Didn't care if we were overheard

You wanted to please me
That was plain to see
Being with you was enough
Me all alone with thee

I'd hang on your every word
Believed everything you said
That's why I'm struggling today
Your words; they took us to bed

Perhaps that was the other one
I've seen two sides of you
The one that loved me; and
The one that made me blue

So why can't I block you off?
Like you did not exist
You don't seem to have a problem
Forgetting the passion in our kiss

Words Weren't Enough

The words
They just won't cease
No matter what I do
There is no release

Day and night
Like being caught in a hail storm
Down they come; and
This poetry they form

You used to tell me
I'd run out of words
To keep writing you poems
That's simply absurd

You had such an affect
Words simply aren't enough
To express how I feel; and
They're not just rough and fluff

Your influence was profound
To say the least
But nothing I did or said
Would stop the eventual grief

I Will Always Love you

My love for you handsome
It hasn't diminished
Although for you
It appears to have vanished

You took what you wanted
Then scurried away
Like a mongrel dog
To love another day

The ocean is plentiful
Of fish and more fish
Well; so I am told; but
That's not my wish

People say you're a bastard
And a rat to boot
They don't know we were lovers
That's why it's such a hoot

To hear other's opinion
So different to mine
They experienced you first hand
And don't rate you kind

So if I had have listened
Would things have been different?
I doubt it but then
I may be indifferent

Once Upon A Time

Once upon a time
Out in the country
There lived a girl
With a frangipani tree

Whilst in the city
There resided a boy
They met and flirted
But he remained coy

Not wanting another regret
She declared to him her love
But it wasn't enough; and
Required intervention from above

Their love won out; and
Put a smile on her dial
He made her so very happy
Alas; it was only for a while

He taught her to love
Then he bid her adieu
And in the flash of an eye
Returned to what he knew

But her love is eternal
And her life it must go on
She prays they get past this; and
Get together again and beyond

The Bush to "The Shire"

She lived near Windsor
He resided at Kirrawee
Their lives were so different
But she couldn't see

They called her 'a bushie'
He came from "The Shire"
But that's not the reason
Him: she did admire

He is so good looking
And gentle of the heart
Not to mention sweet and caring
And that's just for a start

When they were together
The world would stop oscillating
So they could enjoy their time
Without it rapidly abating

Every moment was precious
Each day was a treasure
Loving you handsome
Was such a pleasure

I have only one regret
That you couldn't see
That together with me
You should now be

Vicki Elizabeth

There was a country beauty
Vicki Elizabeth was her name
After you dumped her
Her poetry shot to fame

Her poems tell of love
A love so pure and true
And of a loss so difficult
It killed all of her hue

She writes down her words
To help ease the pain
Retaining beautiful memories
Of a love you just can't fain

Whilst he'll never read them
Many others; they now will
Out there now published
A new chapter they now fill

She dreams of the day however
He comes back to her
And happiness will be reflected
In her poetry then; he'll concur

Until that day comes
Her life will continue
But it will never be the same
If she doesn't have you

What A Fool Are You?

I wanted you handsome
I desired you too
You deserve to be loved
That's all I wanted to do

400 poems now written
350 poems are published
My love and adoration for you
You should not have rubbished

You say you know what love is
But you don't have a clue
Let go of a dream come true
Well; what a fool are you?

One day you will realise
That I really do love you
Realise what you sacrificed
Then what will you do?

Do you have any idea?
How the world is seen
Through a sea of tears
Each day; as my life careens

Two Women's Tears

Sometimes I get so angry
I want to ring your neck
The way you loved then left me
Leaving me an awful wreck

I don't know how many times
I've sat alone and cried
Wondering and pondering
Why my Eros; why?

If I was just a chess piece
On your board game of life
You should have known better
Then to put yourself in strife

Now there are two women
Who now cries for you
Only one can win however
What are you to do?

You could lose them both now
That's another possibility
But whatever happens
Will you take responsibility?

Two Women's Love

Two women's tears
Two women's sorrow
But a woman's heart
A man should never just borrow

Two women cry
A great name for a song
Cry over the same man; and
Two loves that went wrong

Two women love you
Both women care
If you think about this
Is this really fair?

Both women want you
Now they both know
But only upon one should
Your love you bestow

One already has you
The other; wants you so
For a love so deep and true
Will you let the first one go?

You are so very lucky
Two women love you so
But unfortunately for one
One you have to let go

A Lesson Learnt

Do you know?
How handsome you are
I don't think you do
To me you are a star

I thought you were a man
A man who had it all
But you ran to me; and
Upon my love you did call

I didn't have to hide
When I was with you
Just who I really am
You're one of a rare few

We had some great times
I'd call them the best
Especially the hours spent when
I laid my head upon your chest

When you hurt me handsome
You went too far
We would have been safer
Just dancing the Cha Cha

When you play with fire
You have to get burnt
Loving and losing you
Was a lesson learnt?

An SMS Was Easy

Your beautiful eyes
So stunning and green
Are the pathway to your soul
And this; I have seen

This; I believe
Is the reason why
You couldn't look into my eyes
So you SMS'ed goodbye

You knew that I would see
See right through you
Your eyes saying one thing
That your words should say to

An SMS was easy
Your eyes and your words
As well as your voice
By me; not seen or heard

When you left me handsome
I thought that I would die
I spend each and every day now
Trying to understand why

You Unleashed a Poet

Three books now I've written
About my love for you
People say I am talented; and
It's all because of you

You took your time with me
When others didn't care
You unearthed a poet that
With the world you now share

The world has a poet
Who writes of love and love lost
But if she could have you back
She'd pay any asking cost

Show me another woman
Who loves a man as much
And I'll show you someone
With a poetic touch

A poetic flare that comes
From a heart that is true
A heart that was offered you
With no strings placed upon you

Only to see you sometimes
Or hear from you now and then
Affection when and if you could; and
For there to be no pretend

You Found a Treasure

I've always felt very different
The odd one out at least
The 'Ugly Duckling' I epitomised; but
When I met you that all ceased

Within me you found a treasure
That others viewed and left
You recognised a thing of value; and
Realised you had the best

You kept it all to yourself
Admired it when you could
Used it when you shouldn't
Then abandoned it on the hood

What you once cared for
Has gone to wrack and ruin
Left alone to fend for herself
What the hell are you doin'?

Some men search a lifetime
For a treasure like you found
They'd lock it up and treasure it
And without uttering a sound

You had it all
Yet you choose to walk away
Something I'll never understand
Until my dying day

Look to the Future

The past
That we cannot change
But the future
We can definitely rearrange

I'd love to hear your voice
Calling out my name
Hearing that again
Would my love again inflame

Anything that is worth having
Is worth fighting for
How do I convince you?
It's you alone that I adore

I trusted my instincts; and
Presented you with my heart
You strongly affected my life
Right from the very start

You left me wanting you more
You; I absolutely adore
Tell me what I need to do
For you to present at my door

I Am the Lock; You Are the Key

I am the lock
You are the only key
Until we got together
Neither could be set free

Your key was made precisely
To fit exactly into me
We were made to be together
Why can't this you see?

How many times?
Do keys they get lost
Most are never found again; or
Have to be duplicated; at cost

You know where your lock is
As to I; my key
Yet for whatever reason
You walked away from me

Some people search a lifetime
To find a match like ours
A love that is so pure and true
That I promise will never sour

I want you to return to me
Your key in your outstretched palm
So that I know that this time
Me you will not again harm

I am the lock & you are the key

You Inspire Me

Tonight I authored a letter
Addressed to my Guardian Angel
For the information and attention of
My high ranking Archangel

I asked her to tell me
Something I need to know
What is in your heart?
And will I again glow

You inspired me handsome
On oh so many levels
Your love and attention
My feeling always revels

We share a unique chemistry
And I can make you laugh
Without you handsome
I'll forever only be a half

I've never given up on you
Of that I am very proud
I'll never stop loving you; and
To that I also vow

You have to admit
With me by your side
Our love was incredible; and
One hell of a ride

The Dream

My dog he was barking
So I turned around
You will never guess
What my eyes found

You in my driveway
Your heart on your sleeve
Telling me that
You will not again leave

We embraced
As if never apart
Our lives together
We can now start

My reaction to you
It did you astound
As my arms and body
Toward you were inbound

Then my body shook
And I awoke
I was only dreaming
Nigh a word spoke

It was a nightmare
You were not there
So I began crying
But do you even care?

The Words Never Stop

The words
They keep smashing me
Its constant; no relief
Why can't they let me be?

I've never experienced this
With any other before thee
Whether you believe me
It's true; please trust me

I'd never written a poem
Now I've written many hundred
Because my intense love for you
These poems; the words are fed

I can't recall the last night
I've slept right through
The words they tormented me
Until this poem grew

I'll wager you any money
No other has done for you
What I've said, done and written
For you; it's so easy to do

But I'm all alone tonight
You; my love are not
I pray that you are happy
Now with your chosen lot

I'll Never Forget You

What the hell are you doing?
It's been three weeks today
Since you called me last; but
Had very little to say

It's like you're playing games
With my feelings and emotions
Getting some sick pleasure
Reigniting love and devotions

I doubt that you give a thought
To what you are doing
Playing my heart and feelings
Keeping my love stewing

I wish you were lying beside me
Warming me with your body heat
Like you did that cold June night
In that luxurious hotel suite

If all the poems I have written
The gifts, the words and the love
Aren't enough to show you; then
I'll need help from up above

What we had was amazing
Whether you admit it or not
One thing I know for sure
You'll never be forgot

If You Come Back

If one day in the future
You do change your mind
And want to come back to me
I vow that I will be kind

You won't have to worry
About what will greet you
You will always be welcome
Into my heart; that's true

Whether you come to me
Or I run to you
It really doesn't matter
As long as we're together to

No need to utter a word
It won't matter to me
You embraced in my arms
Is all I long to see

Love Has No Ending

Love comes from God
Love is without an end
I thank God I found you; and
To me he did you send

I love you so much
But you don't have any idea
What these words mean
Although them from me you hear

The room is lit with candles
As it was that May night
You came and made love to me
Doing everything just right

You hardly said a word
Your mouth was preoccupied
Creating and enlightening senses
That just never died

I do remember vividly
My hands wanting you so
They couldn't get enough of you
Or a fair go

A woman can search a lifetime
To find that one special guy
But what do you do when
He picks another; ask why?

Our Love is a Guitar

Our love is like
Playing the guitar
You must know what you're doing
If it's going to go far

Just as the guitar strap
Holds the guitar in place
So to do my arms
When you they embrace

Just like your fingers move
For each guitar chord
You fingers explored me
And I had to applaud

As does your voice
It gives the music words
Instead of just music
A love song is now heard

As the music is born
A new song each time
It's like our growing love
And these poems that rhyme

Then the guitar
Is placed in its case
Just like my heart
For you to keep safe

Each guitar is different
Made for a specific purpose
Just like you and I
Not to be alone and surplus

Vicki & her Fender Telecaster guitar

Loving the Wrong Men

What is it?
With men and promises
Words said without thought
And all too ominous

The most important thing
In any man's life
Is not sleeping alone; but
Without getting into strife

Some men will try and use you
For their own sexual purpose
Once it is discovered that
You have been declared surplus

They circle around you
Just like some sick vulture
It is like some
Unwritten male culture

They say that they'll call
And then they don't
They promise they'll see you
But you know that they won't

It's all our own fault
We set ourselves up
Loving the wrong men
Before the ultimate break-up

A Sacred Love

I'm not your average girl
I am the complete package
Not to mention unpredictable
With a chest full of courage

I don't fall in love easily
Nor can I just walk away
Not on a bad note
After with you I did lay

My relationship with you
To me; was so sacred
You are the only one for me
Despite by you; being jaded

I know that I'll never find
That kind of love again
Nor will I subject myself
To the unrelenting pain

But I will always have memories
Memories I would not have had
Had we not shared something
And for that I am so glad

Now I may appear angry; and
To that you're probably right
But you will have to concede
I've been through a rough plight

She's the Winner

I asked you once
If I scared you
To wit you responded 'no'
Then recanted; yes you do

I do not believe
It was fear that you felt
But rather strong feelings
That made your heart melt

I can understand however
That you might feel awkward
Married to one woman; but
For another; feelings toward

It must have been difficult
I don't envy your plight
But in the end; you hurt me
So you could make things right

But the only winner here
Is the one that drove you away
Not you; not I; or
The feelings that made you stray

Now we are both lonely
But alas; she is now content
She has you and what you give her; and
It's her with whom you went

I'm Rich but not Wealthy

I am not considered wealthy
But I am rich in many ways
All of which I'd share with you
For your love until our last days

I can make you happy
In ways you never thought possible
Fresh air; laughter and frivolity
Are on the list of do (able)

People; they look up to me; but
To me; they have so much more
I have family, friends and health
But other than that; I'm poor

So I can't offer to buy your love
I can't match what you possess
All of your material assets
Mine; are worth much less

But what I can offer you
You simply just can't buy
That's a love so deep and true; and
A promise of that until I die

But it is all up to you
I've told you this many a time
There's no other way to tell you
All that I have is yours; and mine

The Female Mantra

Men;
They want it all
The wife, kids, house; and
A mistress secreted in the hall

It's like a badge of honour
Worn proudly around their neck
But you have to watch the mistress
If she says; what the heck!

They forget the female mantra
Get angry; get over it
Then! Get even!!
To us; it's only fit

To men it is all
Ram and bam to do
And if you're really lucky
You may get a 'thank you'

Young girls today they tell me
Fight fire with fire
Go for the jugular; and
Show them out to be a liar

But to me; it isn't right
To make my Eros pay any price
When we were both at fault
The ending; the throw of a dice

I'd Do It All Again

I sent you a love poem
That your wife did see
And less than a week later
You were making love to me

Sometimes; I stop and question
What I see and love in you
When you think about it
This is what you do!

I guess that I am lucky
That she did win out
If you did this to me
I would want to scream and shout

The penalty for me though
It must be the same
Because in reality
We were both to blame

I can put forth excuses; and
Reasons for what we did
But be it right or wrong
In the eyes of God; it's forbid

So I'll take what's coming
As too will you
But if I had my life over
Again; it I would again do

Head and Heart Struggle

My heart tells me it's right
My head tells me it's wrong
The analysis of both is
It's with you that I belong

I hope and pray to God that
What you gave me in the past
Will again manifest itself; and
Lead you back to me; and last

What we did was wrong
But God! it felt so right
I can only stand back and wait; and
Hope you again see the light

A light that's strong and bright
Shining the path back to me
A path that you will run along
Until at the end; it's me you see

Then we can end what we began
A love made in heaven
That's sanctioned and blessed
At the highest reverend

In Utopia
Then we will reside
To love and honour
Side by side

Make the Words Stop

Please!
I beg you
Give me a break
So I can sleep through

It's just gone midnight
Five poems already written
You have to concede
It's love; I've been bitten

I can see an end
To yet another book
I pray that one day
At all three; you take a look

If three published books
Aren't enough to convince you
Of the love that I have for you
I'm at a loss what else to do

The broken sleep
Is slowly killing me
At least there are three books
In the stores for you to see

Regardless of whom you are
You cannot deny my love
I wish I could sent it to you
In a floral arrangement of purple foxglove

My Love in Words

People keep telling me
That time; it heals
But it's been eleven months; and
My heart; it still reels

It's reflected in my words
And in all of my writing
Imagine how much worse it'd get
If there was to be a sighting

People also tell me
I have to ditch the photograph
That sits beside my bed; but
I can't deal with my own wrath

Most people say they've loved
Yet I don't think they've known
Especially a love
Like to you; I have shown

If everyone could love but once
And it be a love like mine and yours
Then people from all over
Would flock to Aussie shores

Yes; you are so very special
Exceptional to say the least
Even though at times
I portray you as a beast

The Sky's the Limit

The sky's the limit
That's what I'm told
I guess time will tell; and
The number of books sold

The sky's the limit
And I'm ready for it
Despite all that's happened
I don't' intend to quit

The sky's the limit
Anyone can reach it
Just give it a try
It will take some grit

The sky's the limit
My love I can't quit
Despite everything
My love I can't twit

The sky's the limit
My feelings won't quit
I could try new things
But not learning to knit

The sky's the limit
You have to have been
To hell and back; if
Its benefits are to be seen

What a Transformation

One hell of a transformation
My family and friends have seen
They can't believe their eyes; and
It's all because with you I've been

There's nothing I don't do now
Nothing I won't give a try
It could have all been yours; and
Without you having to buy

From the lawns to the gutters
And changing light bulbs too
I've even got pretty good at
Polishing paten leather shoes

The gas heater and water leaks
Is no challenge for me
Like 'Rapunzel' locked in the tower
You did release me; you see

People tell me I'm amazing; and
Gone from strength to strength
Since I exiled my 'Ex'; and
A relationship with you did commence

You discovered an amazing woman
Which had been dormant for too long
The only thing I can't do now
Is get you to where you belong

Vicki—Who would have ever believed this?
Photograph by: Nguyen, Luc (04/05/2012)

1 300 EROS

My life is a mess
I don't know what to do
Call 1 300 EROS
If only he knew

When he does call
I don't tell him all
He's having enough trouble
Getting himself over the wall

I am the best friend
He's ever had
He doesn't yet realise
Nor was it some fad

I love you Eros
I love you and care
No contact with you
Is more than I can bear

You deserve so much
And I don't deserve you
Believe me or not
Not more could be truer

I don't hate you
That's my problem
I'd do anything
If you'd return this autumn

Serenity

'Serenity'
Means peace and calm
My life's not been the same
Since we left the farm

You were the first
The first good thing
To happen in my life; and
I didn't need a ring

Although our time was short
It was an amazing ride
Although our feelings
We were forced to hide

My life's seen some crap
I've fought for everything
Even you made me work
Until your head went '*ding*'

You bought my life happiness
You bought my life calm
You made me feel safe
When my hand was in your palm

But since you left me
So too did my serenity
But one thing I don't want
Is any sort of pity

But!

It's such a pity
It took a love; then grief
To realise a talent
That was then unleashed

I've run races on foot; and
Completed them on a steed
But nothing comes close
To my love; you impede

I've studied hard
Earned a degree
But no struggle was harder
Than when you cut me free

I've put myself out there
Suffered heartache and pain
Nothing can compare to that
From you I did sustain

I've given a lot of myself
But no more than to thee
But it wasn't enough
My love; to make you see

I've worked really hard
Even had two jobs at once
But I've never worked harder
Than dealing with your absence

Love!

LOVE; is what I feel for you
ONLY; exclusively mine
VALENTINE; no longer anonymous
ETERNAL; until the end of time

LOVABLE; is what you are
OBJECT; of my desire
VEHICLE; to my happiness
EFFECT; never felt higher

LABYRITH; what you portray
OINTMENT; to my soul
VALUE; your worth to me
EFFORT; lost all self-control

LANGUID; how you left me
OCTOBER; our birthdays
VITAL; to my contentment
ELECTRIC; each and every day

LAME; the way you ended it
OBLIVION; what I am to you now
VERACIOUS; truth; all I expected
EASE; always I vow

LONESOME; now, how I am
ORDEAL; what I am now living
VACANT; how you left my heart
EVER; always forgiving

Some Mock Me

God gave me a gift
That you helped reveal
Discovered in my poetry
Telling you how I feel

It's hard to explain
The words in my head
Even harder to explain; that
They come to me in bed

Different things; well
They set me off
Most people love them
Whilst others; they scoff

Work colleagues mock me
Be it ever so suttle
But who do they run to?
When in a work muddle

All that they say
Doesn't rattle me
I found a great love
That they just don't see

Most wouldn't know love
It if bite them on the arse
That's why their mockery
Is such a farce

Questions

Isn't it funny?
What some people will do
When they think you've got money
And have become a who's who

The question most asked
Is how much I've made
Not how am I feeling since
Being hit with the grenade

The next most inquired
Is the name of my lover
Who is this man?
Whose arse you cover

Only a few friends
Have called to ask
How I am doing so
I don't end up in a cask

I'd give all my money
My gift and my name
If he would come back
And me he did claim

There's nothing else I can do
I've said, done and written
Everything that's possible
To be his little kitten

Mum and Dad

Mum and dad have been great
But they don't understand
The books; the poems; or
The love I have for this man

They're glad that I have found
This creative niche in life
Now they don't have to worry
About me getting into strife

You know
They've never asked
Anything about this man
Within whose love I've basked

I guess they know the answer
Hence no questions needed
And; with no questions
No lies to be conceded

Mum has spoken to him
On my mobile phone
Even cooked us dinner
When he visited my home

They just want me happy
With a man by my side
But as much as I've asked
He simply can't comply

The Other Woman

The greatest disappointment
In my life to date
Was losing you handsome
My amazing soul mate

Although different genders
We are so much alike
From the same birthday; to
Being comfortable behind a mike

Then there's a love of animals
But of horses, the most
But she won't go riding with you
When you vacation up the coast

I doubt she loves music
Like we both do
From jamming on the guitars
And other things we like to

We can't exclude making love
At that you do exceed
You love and keep going
Until I have to ring the bell

But despite all of this
You choose to stay with her
I guess I underestimated
The love within you she stirs

Nothing's Changed

I look at photographs
I've seen of you and her
The appearance of love
They just do not stir

Of all the photos seen
There's nigh a single one
With that look in your eyes
Over here to me; please come

There is always distance
Between both your bodies
And definitely no look
Hey! Want to be naughty

I guess I'm just trying
To convince myself somehow
You came because you wanted to
Looked at me and thought; wow!

If I am honest with myself
You just wanted my body
Because she locked hers away
And I offered mine; a real hotty!

Well; you won for a while
Now you're back where you were
I'm at home alone pining
While you're alone; with her

You Are To Me!

You are the only man
That I want to spend
My remaining life with
And it's no pretend

You are my hero
I miss you so much
You love; your warmth
Not forgetting your touch

You are my champion
I've even asked for
A love song dedication
To tell you; you I adore

We've had months apart
We can never get back
Without you handsome
My life is forever black

I want to give myself
To you; and only you
In every way
What are we to do?

I love you so much
Don't ever question this
I'll always be here for you
If that is your wish

My Country Boy

You're a country boy
Living in the city
Taking you out of the country
Was such a great pity

No prestigious home
Or any amount of money
Can change who you are
It's really quite funny

Until I came along; and
Reignited that country feeling
Suppressed for too long
They sent you reeling

You'll always be a 'Westie'
Although you live else where
No matter how hard you try
You can't change that you care

We'd speak of horses
Pickles and homemade apple pie
Because in your heart
You never said goodbye

Until you sit up and realise
To follow your head and heart
Come back to me in the west
And a great life we'll start

Love Never Ends

Love just doesn't end
Not when it is real
It doesn't matter to you
I'll never change how I feel

Last night
I picked up my guitar
First time in months
I've come so far

The darkness
Is slowly lifting
It's been a long time; and
Its only befitting

Now; looking back
I can see our end
Was a new beginning; and
My heart can begin to mend

My tears,
Are now less frequent
But my love for you Eros
Will always be reverent

So as the shadows fade
And they are no more
A new start beckons; but
Won't mend my heart that's tore

The Fissure

Your love
Opened up a fissure
Released a creative chakra
From which words now pour

The fissure; it grew
And poetry emerged
And ever since then
It has literally surged

The fissure; it is now
A raging volcano
Poetry flows like lava; and
We need a piano

Only time will tell
If this volcano will
Again become dormant; or
Continue to fulfil

Will an event occur?
That caps it off forever
Or; will nothing stop it?
Nothing whatsoever

The Phoenix

Your love
Resurrected me
Once a baron wasteland; now
An oasis; all long to see

There isn't anyone better
For you; than me
I hope and pray
Eventually you see

Walking away from me
Was the worst mistake
You'll ever make
For God's sake

Just like the phoenix
Reincarnated from the ashes
Reborn anew to live again
Resurrected from life's trashes

May the love we shared
Never vanish from your thoughts
It was so amazing
It can never be bought

Trust in your dreams
They're the path to your soul
Trust in them; and
The world is yours to behold

The Journey

With you
I found happiness
After you
I discovered darkness

Since you
I've struggled
Not knowing why
Has left me troubled

My heart beat so fast
The first time I told you
That I loved you
That's what you do

I want to see
The light again shine
In your eyes; and
To; in mine

Mine began to shine
During our first kiss
And from then thereafter
It was total bliss

But now
They are lifeless
And that's how they'll stay
Until me; you again bless

I Wish You Well

It isn't healthy
Holding onto a dream
Waiting for a man; who
To you has been mean

I'm tired of the feeling
Of tears on my cheek
I'm tired of feeling
Oh so very weak

I thought I was over you
But obviously I'm not
But for you however
I'm probably now forgot

I feel so vulnerable
Right here and now
To make things worse
I can't openly avow

You don't want me; and
I am disappointed
Even more so because
Our love we anointed

Regardless of everything
I want you to enjoy bliss
In whatever you do; and
With whomever you wish

No One Will Ever

No one will ever
Fill your existence
The way that I can; but
Not from a distance

You found a seedling
Neglected and needing care
Nurtured it with love; and
Grew a bloom fit to share

You cut your bloom
Kept it all to yourself
When you were done with it
Discarded it to the shelf

Then ran away from me
And did so by stealth
Leaving an amazing love; and
A life filled with wealth

Now neither of us is happy
Despite what you might say
Only you can change this
Don't leave it another day

Eros

Until you've lived in darkness
And see how dark it can be
You must travel there
If ever to really see

Eros was the first man
To whom I've never lied
Opened myself up to him
And ended up deep fried

You get back what you give
That's what we are told
But no one told Eros
Look at how it did unfold

I have known hurt
And what loss can be
I have also known grief
With you; I experienced all three

I never dreamt you'd hurt me
Not for a solitary second
I never saw it coming
So; how am I this to reckon?

The promise you made me
I accepted in good faith
But at the first opportunity
You decamped post haste

The Power of One

We all have to start somewhere
My life truly began with you
It doesn't take much to change a life
That is what you best do

What I experienced with you
Made me sincerely appreciate
The power of love between two
Then me; you did alienate

It is so sad now however
That it is hurt; not love
That now fuels my poems
No longer you my beloved

Imagine what can become
When the hurt is no more
When love again reigns; and
The poetry it does pour

I've been hurt by so many
Men in my life thus far
Will I ever find another?
Who can repair the scar?

The scar etched upon my heart
And the damage to my soul
Only you can this mend
It has taken its toll

Will I Ever?

Will I ever?
Again feel love
A love so deep and true
As it was with you

Will I ever?
Ever truly be free
Free from the affect
You had upon me

Will I ever?
Again know peace
Like lying in your arms
Was a musical caprice

Will I ever feel?
The warmth of your body
Beside me at night
This; I'll always embody

Will I ever?
Make love to you again
There's nothing more beautiful
To that; Amen

Will I ever?
Again be with you
This time for all eternity; and
Never again; an adieu

Two Women's Hearts; Only One Key

Two women's hearts
Only one key
You hold the choice
Which will it be?

You married one heart; and
Borrowed the other
One was your wife; and
The other your lover

You had everything; but
You weren't happy at home
You saw something you wanted
And you decided to roam

You wanted your cake; and
To eat the icing too
You held all the aces
So what did you do?

You held two hearts
In the palm of your hand
When it got too hot
You took off and ran

Now two hearts are hurting
Two hearts now cry
Two hearts are bleeding
And you know why!

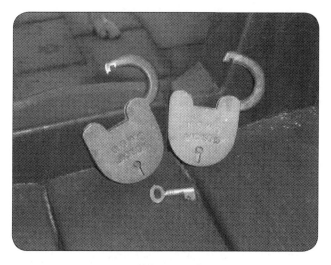

Two women's hearts; only one key

The Wishing Bench

I sit here all alone
Beneath a weeping willow tree
Upon an old stone bench wishing
You were here with me

Leaves; they rain down upon me
As the breeze gently blows
Crying my eyes out
As my emotions; ebb and flow

The bench is sadly weathered
Just like my heart and soul
We've both seen better days
Before our beauty was stole

Sitting here I can see afar
And listen to the river flow
Loving and missing you terribly; and
Wondering if you know

I pray the strength of my hopes
And the depths of my desires
Are conveyed to you in full upon
The wings of my Guardian Angel choir

Old Stone Seat; Ebenezer Church NSW

Yvette

In the mail
Arrived a thank you card
I was truly touched
And caught off guard

Yvette sees my gift
And encourages me
As too did my Eros
He too did see

Yvette is an amazing woman
And in her own right
I am so very fortunate
I was caught in her sight

She too has known a love
A love so deep and true
Just like the love
That I found with you

Yvette really understands
No one can ever replace
Your love and soul mate
Nor can him you ever efface

Yvette; she could
Even be my mother
She's read all my three books
From cover to cover

Eros Opened a Door

Eros; he opened a door
That had been locked forever
He turned on the light; and
Behold; someone whose clever

Eros gave the world
An incredibly gifted writer
Then he ran and fled
Unlike me; he's no fighter

Now the world is blessed
But alas; not the poet
I found poetry but lost my love
And boy; don't I know-it!

There is so much more
From whence this came
What Eros has unleashed
Let no other ever refrain

Sadly; what Eros gave the world
He; no longer sees or reads them
Because he choose to stay at home
And gave up his exquisite gem

My greatest fear now
Is that my poetries potential
Won't be truly recognised until
I am no longer existential

Profound Words of Love

You just don't know
How much it will cost
To get what you want
More so; when it's lost

I look up at the sky
As the clouds they pass by
Images of you are
All I can spy

As the memories flood back
I again began to cry
And again ask myself
Why my beloved? Why?

I love you more
Than at any other time
There's nothing I wouldn't do
If it would make you mine

It's been eleven months now
I've lost a lot of weight
But despite it all
You; I could never hate

Profound words of love
Adorn this poem and page
But the way you left me
They should be words of rage

I'll Love You Forever

I cried again today
Tears I shed for you
Cried; 'til I soaked my pillow
Cried; because there's nothing I can do

When I left a man
My partner of twenty five years
Nigh a tear was shed
Because him; I left in fear

Since I lost you however
The tears they never stop
Losing you handsome
I simply can't cop

I've tried everything
I've prayed to God
I've begged my Angels
But not a sign or a nod

I've even prayed to you
Each and every night
I've never missed one yet
Hoping you'd make it right

I know we have a future
Our future is together
I know I can make you happy
I promise I'll love you forever

The Power of My Words

Why can't people
Just come out
Say what they think; and
What their thoughts are about

Only then will they see
That there is more value
In words said from the heart
Then by the tongue; impromptu

I have published my words
So they might reach you
One day you will realise
What you need to do

The words in my poems
Come from my bleeding heart
The power of my words
Come from us being apart

To a beautiful paradise
You lost the key
It was lost the day
You walked away from me

I've been infatuated before
But I've never loved like this
I wait the day handsome
You retrieve me from the abyss

My Vow

To my beloved Eros
The following to you I vow
The promises I'll etch in blood
If this you will allow

I promise to always love you
I promise I'll love you forever
With a love that's deep and true
And that I'll leave you never

I promise you my heart
Carried on a silver tray
From now until eternity
Until my last day

I promise you my soul
For it is nothing without you
Do with it as you wish
It is yours to possess too

I offer you my body
Although it's done some mileage
It will serve you well; and with it
You have freedom of passage

I promise you my loyalty
I promise to never forsake
No other could be more faithful
And a beautiful life we'll make

Finally; my home and chattels
Will become your kingdom
Of which you will be King
There to live your life in freedom

My Beloved Eros

The love that I found with you was the most fulfilling of my life.
I love you more than I ever envisaged possible.
I will always love you, no matter what.
I beg you to find your way back to me.

Gorgeous xxx

Dream you dream to the sky and it will bring you your beloved
Kahlil Gibran '*Sand & Foam*'

Vicki Case; Author. Photograph taken by; Nguyen, Luc (June 2012)

Unconditional Forbidden Love (cover)

A Journey of Hurt; Captured in Ink (cover)